Contents cont'd

Contents cont'd

Dedication

My Mother, Father, Lesley and Joanne

My Hayley and Harvey

(I'm sorry for the lost years)

Christine Nicholson

(You saved my life)

The staff at Addenbrookes Hospital

Kevin Nutt my solicitor

Victim Support

Headway

Combat Stress

Lorna Day my social worker

(I'll never forget the five pounds)

My friend Judith Smith

Grace Lures

My dear Claire

Sharon Elliot

Colonel Robbie Robinson (SSAFA Forces Help)

Sandra (For holding me in your arms)

My assailant whom I forgave all those years ago

I will Never forget you all.

Acknowledgements

I wish to thank the Airborne Forces Security Fund for generously funding the money for this project.

You have done me well.

Thank you

Joey Joe McGuire

Foreword

Do poets get better and wiser as they get older? I'd like to think so. You'll notice that I have arranged the poems in date order so you can judge for yourself. I think that poems can be a reflection of your inner self at the time of writing. Every poem is special. It matters not who wrote it or its content, only that someone has felt the need to sit down and write it at the time. What better gift for a loved one than your own original poem. What better tool to express yourself in a public place. Poems can be left behind forever when you are long gone. Something for your nearest and dearest to hold on to as they mourn your loss. With poetry you can say anything you want. People will laugh, cry, understand and even agree with you sometimes. Even the hardest soul can be touched at some point in their lives. Poetry is for everyone and I believe, as I would, that it will be the recreation of the future.

This is my first book and is the prelude to my first novel 'A State of Mind (The Novel') which hopefully will be available next year.

A State Of Mind

Where's my mother, is she sleeping, her little boys in pain. Does she know that I am crying? Does she know that I'm alone at night? Can she feel my presence so far away, my soul searching for help? In the darkness I am weeping, in the darkness of the day, in the darkness of the night, it's all the same. Where's my mother, does she know me, does she lie awake and wonder, what I have become, what has become of me? Where's my mother is she sleeping, does she hear me call her name, does she know I have a new friend called the loneliness of night?

Along the pathways I have found, the pathways where I wander, there is no one. There is darkness in the daylight, there are rooms with bolted doors, there are faces without features, there is no sound along the pathways, where I linger, where I tread. There are no living creatures; dead are the souls who linger, in the darkened crevasses, where they hide. Where's my mother is she sleeping, please protect me, for I am lost, for now I am lost. Hear me calling for my mother, hear my voice upon the winds, the winds on which I travel, the silent winds of darkness, the winds of day and night.

My friend is called the stranger, the stranger of the night. He never talks, not a word uttered, he has no lips, she has no eyes. There are no features that I can define, that I can describe. Never talks to me, never a word is spoken, only listens to my crying, only listens to my bleating, never talks, never makes a sound, only listens to my crying. I never see him, she is hiding, in shaded corners, darkened crevasses, in the night and also in the daytime, only listens to my crying, sleeping mother can you hear me, I am calling you tonight.

There are no clocks upon the walls along the pathways where I tread. No silent ticking, no passing minutes, there are no days, there are no nights. There are no reasons, no distinctions in the silence, no echoes, no sounds of footsteps, only the hushed silence of the winds, on which I travel with the stranger of the night. No sounds of laughter, no signs of mirth, no rays of sunlight, just endless pathways, with no direction, endless pathways, no direction, pointing fingers on outstretched darkened limbs show the way, but with no direction in the darkness of the night. Where's my mother, is she sleeping, can she hear my cries tonight, does she know that I am dying, does she know that I sleep but do not slumber, no loving arms to hold me, for me the company of a stranger, the darkened figure, he never talks, she only listens, of the stranger of the night. There are rivers from my crying, I cannot see them, but I am aware that they are there. I ask the stranger, can he help me, he is my only friend, she never answers, I go on crying, flooding tears, there is no end without the answers, I ask the questions, I call the tune, but I am lost, along the pathways, in the darkness, alone, except for my one friend, the stranger of the night. Open your window dear mother, there is a message on its' way, slowly drifting with the winds on which I travel, you'll have to listen carefully to the message on the winds. Hushed and whispered are the words, creeping towards you in the night, confused without direction, no guidance given, from the stranger in the night. Hear my cries oh sleeping mother, I sleep alone tonight, there's no-one out there, no one to hold me, I hear voices, no they are whispers, listen carefully sleeping mother, for my cries are on their way.

(A victim of serious violence in 1990 I had finally reached my lowest ebb. I was so alone, vulnerable and isolated. Suicide seemed the only exit from my cul de sac and writing this I feel stopped me doing just that.)
Joey Joe McGuire 1995

Dedicated to the one I love

Come all ye bonnie lads and lasses
To sing and dance with me
For I'm full of airs and graces
For a girl so fair and free

I love to see her roaming
O'er fields and country lanes
Even though she's always telling
Me, I'm oh, so awful vain

Her eyes are filled with glory
Of the days when she was young
When she used to feel so sorry
At the setting of the sun

She tells me of her past
In Corbridge where she lived
Where she'd make her jeans just last and last
For no one really cared

You'd like her if you saw her
I'm confident you would
You'd only need to hear her speak
To know that she's kind and good

To me her lips are tender
As though made of cherry wine
And please God will you bless her
For she's all, all mine

And daisies are her treasure
And buttercups her gold
And she is all the pleasure
I can ever hope to have or hold

I thank you Mother Nature
For a girl so sweet and nice
But why this awful torture
Of a temper I despise

Or shall I say a stubbornness
Which fills her thriving body
Without this she'd be a sweet princess
But then I suppose she'd be snobby

Soon I go to America
And then our love will stop
But in my heart I'll leave her
A sweet Forget Me Not

This poem I'll read to a friend some day
When I am really sad
And at the end, holding it to my heart I'll say
'This is dedicated to the one I love.'

Joey Joe McGuire 1968
(My first Love, My first poem, aged 13)

First Love Hurts

What is this attraction
That takes my love from me
This unnecessary friction
Which is making my heart bleed
Is it just my imagination
Or is it really true
That my heart has palpitations
Every time I think of you.

Is there some kind of medication
Which will make the past a blank
Some sort of medieval potion
That from my soul will yank
The misery of knowing you
The heartbreak you have left
Or do I have to drown my sorrows
In myself for some years yet.

Praise God if this is your notion
Then I think it's right to tell
You that I'd rather join the sinners
With old Lucifer in Hell.

Joey Joe McGuire 1968

Puala Tiomin

Let the sea take my boat
To Puala Tiomin
I am bound from Mersing
For Puala Tiomin
I have left everything
For Puala Tiomin

A dream in the sea waiting for me
Untouched and free, coconut trees
I reach out my hands and touch golden sands
Take me to the land of Tiomin

Puala Tiomin please wait for me
I'm so far away across seven seas
And my heart fills with pain when I come back again
To my home far away from Tiomin

Puala Tiomin ... ...Puala Tiomin ... ...

Joey Joe McGuire 1975

(Tiomin made me decide to leave the Army)

<u>Soldiers Lament</u>

Spare a thought for a man like me
Who'll surely die in world war three
Medals don't make memories
Spare a thought for a man like me

Spare a thought for a man like you
Who gave his life in world war two
Atrocities they made him do
Spare a thought for a man like you

Spare a thought for a man long gone
Who gave his life in world war one
Slaughtered by his brothers gun
Spare a thought for a man long gone.

Joey Joe McGuire 1978
(For Private's Borrucki and Snowdon)

Put out the Lights

Put out the lights and come to bed with me
Draw to the curtains so the world can't see
Put out the lights and we will drift to ecstasy
For I'm in love with you
Only you
Show me the woman, warm gentle woman
I will show you the man, soft tender man
Put out the lights and we will drift on a San Pan
For I'm in love with you
Only you
All my life I can't explain
Why when we're making love it seems to rain
Showers of roses relieve the pain
For I'm in love with you
Only you.

Joey Joe McGuire 1978
(Will Joey get Married?)

Falling in Love

I know when I touch you
You want me
I know when I look at you
You need me
I can feel every heartbeat you make
For it has taken all the pain
Any heart can take
And I know you'll be mine
One fine day.

Joey Joe McGuire 1979?
(Such Passion!)

She Just Learned To Live

You can keep your disco sounds
Going round and round and round
'Cos I have found my feet
Without the beat
Now I'm on solid ground
There'll be no more sordid scenes
Or dates with limousines
No more rides out to the penthouse
For sleazy midnight dreams
For I have found a man who needs me
Wants to change the world to please me
No more midnight hours
Tonight he gave me flowers
And he wants me to have his baby
I am spinning, I am crazy
I have jumped from the merry go round
Don't need music ... ... Don't need sound.

Joey Joe McGuire 1979

I First Met You

There's a little stream on a hillside
Seems to vanish then reappear
There's a hole on distant mountain
Meets the stream where it appears
No one knows just where it starts
No one knows of its fame
But if you listen hard you'll hear the echo
From the distant hole it came.

I first met you
Where the stream went away
And I'd like to meet you at its journey's end
Far, far away ... ...

Joey Joe McGuire 1979?

Black or White (It's all the same to me)

I'm a minority
And for me my life can be so very hard
I've tried all my life to see through clouds of reality
Just to face tragedy from the very start
No man in town cares if I'm around
Nobody cries if I am to die
My ebony skin seems to nurture within a cultured shame
My black curly hair seems to catch peoples stare
As a lion is tamed
I will survive my brothers still alive
I'll search within
The power over sin
I'll call on my faith in the whole human race
For the world to change
I'll fight every fight, as is my human right
Until humanity's shamed
I will survive my brothers still alive
I'll search within the power over sin ... ...

Joey Joe McGuire 1980?

Beautiful Thoughts

Like a waterfall

A thundering crescendo

Misty water patterns

Hide the image through my window

And through the pouring rain

The sun comes shining through

A ray of golden fortune

Just for me and you.

Joey Joe McGuire 1980?

Say a Prayer

Say a prayer for Argentina
Let us pray for Cambodia
Say a prayer for little children
Let us hope they go to heaven
Say goodbye to nuclear wars
Say goodbye to super powers
No more sunshine through the rain
Only dark clouds pouring pain
Say a prayer for Argentina
Let us pray for Cambodia
Say a prayer for little children
Pray to God they go to heaven.

Joey Joe McGuire 1982
(Written during the Falklands War)

Together

Together we're forever
Together we will be
Together we're a miracle
For everyone to see

Together through the darkest nights
Together holding hands real tight
Together when things aren't so right
Together on our wedding night

We'll be together every day
Together in our simple ways
Together through our lives we'll see
A baby born for you and me

And every year upon this night
My arms around you holding tight
I will ask you if we'll be
Together through eternity

Together we'll live endlessly
Not two as one just you and me
Together we'll build happiness
With my wife I must confess

Together we're forever
Together we will be
Together we're a miracle
For everyone to see ... ...

Joey Joe McGuire March 1982
(We lost Michele but Hayley was on her way)

Falklands Fiasco (1982)

Countdown by the media
Countdown to hysteria
Countdown seeks to reinforce
Puts us on destruction course
Ten, Nine, Eight
Countdown time it's now too late
Eat the dirt don't hesitate
Seven, Six, five
All the mums and dads will cry
And pray to God you're still alive
Four, Three, Two, One
Countdown time it's now all gone
Better get your Tommy Gun
Zero, Zero, Zero, Zero
Zero means the bubble's blown
When will our soldier boys come home
Countdown by the media
Countdown to hysteria
Countdown seeks to reinforce
Puts us on destruction course.

Untitled (1983?)

There's a person in all persons
Whether they are young or old
Firmly wrapped behind a curtain
Unknown secrets left untold.
Closets holding answers
To recollections of the past
Maliciousness and rumours
Smothered under wraps.
Bars to block the windows
Bolts to lock all doors
Invincible the barriers
To hide the secrets we abhor.
Person inside person
Incarcerated pain
Arguing the balance
Let me out I'm not insane.
Answers to all questions
Hidden under wraps
Fears miss the moments
Am I right or wrong... .....Perhaps!

I Beg

I'm begging you now please don't hurt me
Don't hurt me anymore
I know what I've done and I've been wrong
Don't hurt me anymore
Don't walk out that door and leave me crying
One woman one man there's no denying
I'm begging you don't hurt me anymore

Without love there's no pain
Without pain there's no love
And the heavens will rain
Until you come back again

Don't walk out that door and leave me crying
One woman one man there's no denying
I'm begging you don't hurt me
Anymore.

Joey Joe McGuire 1984

Once Only Flowers

Once only flowers there used to be
Now they are dying for you and for me
Ten thousand rainbows engulfed our shores
Now only shadows pave every floor

You're not the light that shines in the night
Yours aren't the hands that are holding real tight
You're not the person, once I have told
I love you
And now you're ever so cold

Lost is the angel once I adored
Lost is the passion once I explored
Now only feelings of being ignored
But I still love you
And now you're ever so cold

Once only flowers there used to be
Now they are dying for you and for me... ...

Joey Joe McGuire 1985

Love Affair

Rushed secret meetings reeking with sin
So few moments together, so much to get in
Hiding in corners, liasons by night
Loud bells ringing, hearts beating with fright
Passions awoken
So few words spoken
Vows that are broken
Letters for tokens

Dreams of a future together are dreamed
Alone the same dreams are not what they seem
Caring for others decisions are hard
Life is a bother, please play the right card
Leave him, deceive him, whatever will be
As long as you spend what's left with me.

Joey Joe McGuire 1985?

Everyone's Involved

Why have you brought me here, it's not my turn to die
Why have you brought me here, it's not a sin to cry
I know I'm not a pretty sight, but I've been here before
She's not the first girl in my life to walk out of the door
Yes of course it was my fault I've driven her away
As long as I can take the pain then it's not for you to say
Maybe she'll come back, when I've cried all my tears
Leaving is one thing, but you can't wash away the years
Maybe I'm a jerk, I've heard it all before
I tried hard to tango, it needs two upon the floor
Suppose I really need this lecture, I've messed it up again
No need to slap me around the ear, I haven't go a brain
Needless to say I'm sorry, don't look at me that way
Just speak your mind and hurry, I haven't got all day
Yes I've tried her number, it's a disconnected line
I know that you are bothered but she's not your wife, she's mine.

Joey Joe McGuire 1985

Stand By Me

I stood by you through the bad times
Held your hand through the pain
Thoughts of me forever gone
In those days when it rained and rained

And don't forget that I'm the man
Who made you what you are
And don't forget I'll always love you
Even from afar

These hard years they have broken
A love that used to be
But all these years I've spoken
In truth and honesty

And I know that I'm not the man
That I used to be
Now there's no shoulder there to cry on
Baby can't you see

Stand by me in my darkest hour
Help me win this fight
I promise you my love will shower
The bad times out of sight

Don't leave me now here on my own
Don't walk out on me
I stood by you and now it's time
For you to stand by me.

Joey Joe McGuire 1986?

Don't Laugh At me 'Cos I'm a fool

Before you I'd lost my way
And all my dreams had gone astray
And please don't laugh at me when I say
I'm here to stay
So don't send me away

I know that I'm a fool
But look what I've been through
How many men can truly say
They've lived my life and lived another day

If you listen I will show you
I'm not a macho man
I'm just a warm gentle lamb
If you're hungry I will feed you
Love and kisses because I need you
And because I do love you.

Joey Joe McGuire 1988?
(Joey finds new love)

From A Daughter In Coma To Her Mother

When I was a child I was blessed with a smile
That you gave me for keeps to greet those I'd meet
You gave me my heart and you gave me my soul
And watched as I relished obtaining my goals.

So mama don't weep and try hard to sleep
For I need you right now, all in one piece
Protecting my space and tying my lace
Smiling your smile into my face.

Remember with pride when I was a child
One moment I'd laugh the next I would cry
I'd pick myself up when I'd fallen down
It was never too hard when you were around

So mama don't weep, my love is for keeps
And I need you to be right next to me
If I do not smile just wait for a while
And I will come home where I really belong.

When I was a child a tyrant and wild
I'd need you along because you were strong
If I had a choice of where I could be
It's here with you nursing and caring for me.

So mama don't weep and try hard to sleep
For I'm not in pain and I'll smile again
Please just be grateful that I'm still alive
With your strength and mine I'll surely survive
If it were you instead of me
There would not be strength just tragedy.

When I was a child it's not hard to say
That you were my life of each waking day
And if it's to be that it's my turn to die
All through your life I'll be by your side.

So mama don't weep and try hard to sleep
For I need you right now all in one piece
Protecting my space and tying my lace
Smiling your smile into my face.

Joey Joe McGuire 1991 (For Christine)

Thoughts After The Axe

Like a fool I walked through life blind I could not see
The evil that was lurking in every shadow around me
I didn't see the knives until they bit into my back
I didn't feel the tongues that twisted all the facts
Believing all was good I missed life's' golden rule
And walked around with eyes shut I must have looked a fool.

Hands came up from the ground, pulled my ankles down
I tried to save myself, to keep my head above the ground
No one there to help me, left to be alone
Drowning in the misery in a sea of rotten bones
And my life had passed by me, an open book for all to see.

I should have looked around in the silence with no sound
I should have heard the tremors of the whispers underground
I should have felt the lurking of the shadows at my back
And the gnawing from the sewers of the millions of rats
And my life had passed by me....An open book for all to see.

Joey Joe McGuire 1991

(My life devastated through head injury, a victim.)

Visit To Brontes' House

I went to Brontes' house
The day before today
I felt a presence in my heart
I hope it's there to stay
I felt the yesteryears sweep by
With waves of deep remorse
And a light shone on my poorly life
To put me back on course.

Joey Joe McGuire 1991

Silly Thoughts

I'm the most consistent man of inconsistency
Consistent in the way I live my life of tragedy
It's not too hard to live a life of happiness you see
But I'll weary through my dreadful days in inconsistency.

Joey Joe McGuire 1991

A Cry From Inside

Don't look away, don't look away
Don't look away from me
Don't turn your head, don't hide your face
Don't look away from me.
My body is a vessel that cherishes my soul
I swear I'll die this moment if you turn away and go
Hold my hand and touch me, my blood does not run cold
I'm living, I am breathing, there's still hope that I'll grow old.
So, don't walk away, don't walk away
Don't look away from me
Don't turn your head, don't hide your face
Don't walk away from me.
My eyes are glazed I cannot speak
Things don't look good for me
But I've been saved although I'm weak
It's still me can't you see.
Don't look away, don't look away, don't walk away from me
Don't turn your head, don't hide your face
Don't look away from me.

Joey Joe McGuire 1992? (Suicidal)

Wake Up Danny Dreamer

I dreamed I'd write a novel or a song
Thought I'd be a righter of all wrongs
Plant some seeds to grow amongst the weeds
Maybe even sail the seven seas
But it's not to be for Danny Dreamer, not for me.
I thought I'd walk the deserts in my life
Climb a mountain 'til I'm out of sight
Lift a ton, run a marathon
But it's not to be for Danny Dreamer, not for me.
I thought I'd have a palace in the sky
Be a prince and rule with love not lies
I'd banish hate to save the human race
But all dreams they turned to nightmares
Now Danny Dreamer only cries.
Now Danny Dreamers crying with real pain
Gone and missed the bus, now it's to late to catch the train
Flight plans gone I'm heading off the rails
Too late to save the dying, now it's to late to save the whales
For Danny Dreamers busy dreaming other dreamy dreams to fail.

Joey Joe McGuire 1992

<u>Untitled</u>

I wasn't born with smiling eyes
They slapped me and they made me cry
I wasn't destined to be tall
God gave me life and made me small
I didn't know how life would be
The whole world filled with cruelty
And in my innocence at birth, my raw naivety
I didn't know the destiny, life had in store for me.
I grew with guidance, being led
Listened to what others said
Tried to understand and be, perfect in entirety
I didn't bully, didn't steal
Developed feelings that were real
I didn't realise it seems
My way of life was just a dream.
But now my adult eyes they see the world is full of tragedy
With everybody at high speed, filled with hatred, gripped by greed
And how I wish that I could meet some kind soul just like me
To walk through life and hold my hand, and always comfort me.

Joey Joe McGuire 1994

To Someone Special

Lift up your head my eyes will be there to greet you
Reach out your arms and mine will be there to hold you
Close both you eyes and I will be there as your guide
Lay down to rest, I will always be by your side
Open your heart, truly mine will carry the burden for us both
Bare all your soul and I will give you missing hope.

If you are brave, I will be fearless by your side
In your darkest moments you'll have me in which to confide
Give me your trust and I'll make the world seem a safer place
Share with me your love and I'll put a smile back on your face
If you hold me closely we can live as one
When all these things come easy true love has begun.

Joey Joe McGuire 1994
(Fighting for his sanity)

At Last You Go Home

Back to the roots
Of an old English town
Where in your youth
You played to the sound
Of the clatter on the cobbles of the peddlers' cart
Learning affairs and matters of heart
The New Year is dawning
It's so good to see
The return to the womb
Of my Geordie family
Newcastle is waiting
As it always does
With its' heart of an empire
And its' wings of a dove
An era has ended
Another begun
Here's to the future
From your loving son.

Joey Joe McGuire 1994

Burr Hole

I have a little friend
Burr Hole is her name
She lives in Bedford now
But Sunderland's whence she came
She has a little twitch
It's called a petit mal
But since she's been at Headway
She's always been my pal
She doesn't often venture
Far away from home
Now she comes to Headway
She's never on her own
She's often heard to prattle on
As many women do
Since she's been at Headway
She really has come through
Every day I see her
She sits and spins a yarn
She's always there amongst us
Down on the funny farm!

Joey Joe McGuire 1994?

Deep Thoughts (Joey Joe McGuire 1995?)

Only shadows left to dance with me
Silent footsteps echo endlessly
Just the whispers of those memories gone
Seems like years that I've been on the run
Try to tell myself the end is nigh
Heartbreak in itself will pass me by
A rope to hang by waits invitingly
An abstract image of my destiny
Empty heartbeats pound within my soul
No flesh to comfort me as I grow old
Alone to walk on through my loneliness
Searching through a haze for happiness
A single shadow lies upon the floor
Catching tears from my eyes that pour
The telephone it never rings
A letter box with rusty springs
From the past images that cloud my eyes
My memory struggles, truth or lies
What's gone by seems stupid now
Things that mattered, ugly rows
Alone, alone it's plain to see
The hand that destiny has given me.

Choices (Joey Joe McGuire 1995?)

One weary path to tread
Short time living, long-time dead
Two paths at every turn
Reasoned judgements, lessons learned.
Each with a choice to make
Well planned outcomes, quirks of fate
One mans rise, another's' demise
Choices made with open eyes
Fictions, factors, lies instead
Grasping, twisting, hanging threads
Running, scurrying, lost and found
Missing people walking round
A sigh, a cry, a passer-by
An alibi to justify
History changed at speedy rate
One mans choice, another's fate
Hearts beat in time with time
God gave this life of mine
One life to call my own
To share with others, be alone
One weary path to tread
Short time living, a long time dead.

More Than A Friend

More than a friend you make me calm
There when I'm lonely to keep me warm
More than a friend you're by my side
Talking so gently when I cry
Sharing the darkness down paths where I tread
Shaking my consciousness back from the dead
Giving me supper when I'm hungry and cold
More than a friend until we are both old
Sharing and caring, giving and kind
Belonging to no one you're special and mine
More than a friend you rock me to sleep
In my heart a memory of you I will keep
Not here to judge or make moral stand
Just there as my mountain when life's out of hand
More than a friend what can I give
My thanks and my love for as long as you live.

Joey Joe McGuire 1995?

Oh Africa

Forget me not Africa
For I am your seed
Sown so young
Who left before
My fruits were borne
Still to return
To see your dawn
Oh continent so vast
Will good fortune
Cross our paths
My bones grow weak
But my heart stays strong
Oh Africa
You are my soul
You are my home
Where I belong.

Joey Joe McGuire 1995?

<u>Love Not Right</u>

And in the midst of all mankind
Lay two weak souls
Both growing old
At different poles
Hating but yet loving
No spoken word
Yet thoughts of mind
Knitted through all eternity
Never to forget
The memory of each other
And the times shared
In each other's arms.
Unforgiving, both not living
Destined for a loneliness
Deeper than the deepest well
Darker than the darkest hell
Walking on this living earth
Two lonely souls, alone since birth.

Joey Joe McGuire 1996

The Jaws Of Death

And in the jaws of death I'd walked
Running scared, often stalked
Day and night crowding in
No shelter from all mortal sin
Running scared, filled with fright
Darkness lurking, onset of night
Running scared, howling winds
Sharp is the air that darkness brings
And death had been a breath away
Lurking, waiting for its prey
And in the jaws of death I'd found
No hiding place, no sacred ground
Then I reasoned with it all
Death comes to creatures' great and small
And even if a breath away
Life must be lived from day to day.

Joey Joe McGuire 1996

Limbo

Ere the night draws in
A cold mist descends
A crawling cloak, so cold... ...so dim
Slowly, slowly time passes by
No stars to light the evening sky.
The wintry dawn seems far away
No shrieks, no cries
The chilling silence of the night
Hanging ...by its' thread...here to stay
Nothing stirs the midnight air
And there am I
Alone with my loneliness... ...
Complete despair.
And many nights had passed this way
Long, long nights and longer days
Existing, hardly living
Like the night, hanging by its' thread
There am I....the walking dead.

When winter bows its' ugly head
Draws its' final gasp
And spring emerges through a haze
Shortening the evening hours
Filling fields with tiny flowers
Will I find my peace at last.
Or will the days replace the nights
Will the hours linger, poised .... perilously
Daring not too quicken
For fear of losing just one second
God forbid.....just one second.
Ere the wintry night draws in
Here I sit... alone
Waiting... ...
Dreaming of an early spring.

Joey Joe McGuire 1996
(Left to rot away on social security for 7 years by CICB)

Touch Me In The Morning

Touch me in the morning
Whisper while it's dawning
All the things I want to know
Say you'll never let me go
Touch me oh so gently
Side by side lay by me
Stroke me with your lips
Thrill me with your kiss
Let me feel your breath upon me
Stop me feeling oh so lonely
Touch me in the morning
Stay with me 'til day is dawning
Touch me in the morning
Wake me as the birds are calling.
Touch me in the morning
In the morning touch me
As the sun does rise above us
Let us fill our hearts with joy
Oh touch me in the morning
In the morning touch me.

Joey Joe McGuire 1996

Confusion

Voices in my head, playing dead, someone said
Mirrors in my mind, reflecting rhyme, keeping time
Drumming in my ears, guarding fears, making tears
Flushing of my cheeks, revealing secrets that I keep
Twitching in my eye, frowned upon by passers-by
Shaking of my voice, uncontrolled, I have no choice
Pimple on my nose, as it shows I am exposed
Thoughts within my brain, I disdain, am I insane
Pounding in my heart, not so smart, from the start
Leaving of my soul, I am told growing old
Shadow on the ground, sun goes down
It's not around.

Joey Joe McGuire 1997
(Medication)

How Silly Love Can Be

I've never seen a rainbow
In the moonlight sky
Nor glimpsed a shining star
In the morning sky so high
I've never lived a minute twice
Nor wished my time again
Never seen a mountain cry
Nor heard a dumb man sing
I've never seen the summer snows
Nor seen a shrinking violet grow
An endless tale I've never heard
Nor seen the flight of wingless birds
I've never heard a silent scream
Nor woken from a loving dream
Never ended at the start
Nor cured the aching in my heart
But every time I look at you
A miracle comes shining through
You take my silly absurd thoughts
And put my life right back on course.

Joey Joe McGuire 1998

Love Letter To My Beloved Grace

I count the seconds ticking by within my heart
And cry with every moment that we are apart
I treasure every memory that I have of you
And know the way I feel my feelings must be true.
Every day that I'm alone my heart is filled with pain
When I look out from my window all I can see is rain
Each night I listen to you sing tears fill my eyes
And I wonder how much more time has to pass me by
Until the day is with me, the day that I'm with you
And look up to the skies to see the sun is shining through
When I can hold you in my arms and show you all my love
And whisper in your ear the words I'm dreaming of
If God is watching over me he'll send you here Right Now
Scented, gift wrapped with a posy and I would tell you how
Much I've longed for, How much I've missed
The soft and gentle feeling of your warm and tender kiss.

Joey Joe McGuire April 1998

(I wish I knew where you are)

With My Sympathy ... To An Old Friend

I wept and I wept 'til the old man died
I wept and I wept then I cried
There was no one outside there to give me a hug
The day that my old man died.

And I don't know why I care
I do not understand
Why it was him and not me
But I do understand, with my heart in my hand
That his life was meant to be

And while he's at peace
And his heart doesn't beat
And his memory just lingers on
I promise him this, after deaths final kiss
That my love will go on and on.

Joey Joe McGuire 1999

Nobody Likes War

Nobody likes war
The paratrooper cried
All his friends were terrified
Their eyes all white and wide

There are no heroes in a war
The paratrooper claimed
Just lost souls gone forever
And those that's left are maimed

I didn't want to go to war
The paratrooper sobbed
His manhood taken from him
Heart and boyhood robbed

Don't make me fight in Vietnam
Nor dig my grave in old Siam
For I am glad that I am home
From where I never wish to roam.

Joey Joe McGuire 1999

Kosovo

I can see the fires burning in the state of Kosovo
Lessons not yet learned from the wars of long ago
I can feel the desperation in all the eyes I see
Another bloody chapter, a nation on its' knees.
I can hear the cries of children, women and the old
If not from broken hearts they die from hunger and from cold
And when the war is over and they've lost their dignity
Will they thank us for our help and our misplaced charity
To me there's just one answer, it's been there since time began
Let the whole world be one nation let's make a brotherhood of man
And anyone that doubts me I challenge you to say
That the way it's always been is the one and only way
Oh Kosovo I cry for you, but you won't be the last
For tomorrows bloody future is the history of our past.

Joey Joe McGuire

(Written during the conflict in Kosovo 1999)

Oh Lady Di

I remember the day Lady Di passed away
Just sheer disbelief from the news in the street
Our nation stood still
And our hearts they did fill
And the tears in our eyes
Were for our Lady Di

But although we all mourned
She created a bond
And with her memory prolonged
We will carry on

Oh Lady Di I will not forget
And for you from my heart I will sing
And remember with pride
And a tear in my eye
My Princess, My beautiful thing... ... ...

Joey Joe McGuire September 1999

Blessing From A Friend

One God to witness one couple stand
In this tiny church, hand in hand
Two golden rings form two endless lines
Bonding them together 'til the end of time
All here are gathered to see their joy
The ultimate dream of a girl and boy
Let's sing hallelujah for their chosen way
To be forever united on their wedding day
God give them hope that their lives will be fine
Through their journey together 'til the end of time
Let all the congregation rejoice aloud
And open your hearts as they make their vows
Glory, glory, glory, witness today
This tender loving couple has chosen their way.

Joey Joe McGuire 1999

<u>**To My Friends**</u>

Doctors and nurses, politicians alike
Telling me how I should live my own life
Scientists, teachers, businessmen too
Clerics and elders to name but a few
You sit at my table drinking my wine
Distorting your faces, you're no pals of mine
You take of my best with little return
Portraying you're caring, with little concern
I watch as you travel your lives planned ahead
No thoughts for the living, no thoughts for the dead
You spit out your lectures by day and by night
Telling me always I'm wrong and your right
You sit by my side in splendour and wealth
But in a room full of people I'm all by myself
Don't stand at My graveside pretending to be
In front of your friends, who are all just like me
At my wake I'll be watching from my place up above
When drunk you profess your undying love

Alone I have travelled, alone I must die
If there's one friend amongst you I'll allow you to cry
He was a bit of a poet, a strange little man
Kept saying things all of us could not understand
Sat in the corner, alone in the end
Drinking his lager, his only friend
Bit of a shame, poor old drunk
Had so much to offer over wine and lunch.

Joey Joe McGuire November 1999
(Getting rid of the anger in order to move on)

Sadness

Why did the world let me down
Just when my chips were down
Why did your faces all turn away
In those days when my chips were down

I travelled the oceans near wide and far
I gave heart and soul for you
But when it was my turn to ask for some love
I was left on my own with the blues

Oh why did the world let me down
Why was there no one around
All of your brave hearts all turned away
In those days when my chips were down.

Joey Joe McGuire December 1999
(I remember the night very well)

1st Millennium Poem

I wonder if you realise while you slept last night
A thousand years had passed us by as the sun gave light
A thousand years of sunshine, a thousand years of rain
A thousand years of pure delight, a thousand years of pain.

I wonder if you realise that on this special day
We all lived through millenniums and carried on our way
I wonder if you realise millenniums passed before
The next millenniums waiting, knocking on our door.

A thousand years will pass, a thousand years go by
But you won't count a thousand years before you have to die
A million, a billion, millenniums gone before
Endless thousand years ... maybe even more ....

Joey Joe McGuire 28th December 1999

2nd Millennium Poem

If I could choose my place to die a poppy field would be
The place I'd rest my weary head for all eternity
I'd sleep with brave men long forgot who'd died with dignity
And hope their dead souls gave me grace
And saved a place for me
If I could choose my time to die my death would surely be
A fitting time to say goodbye to all who'd cherished me
And if the future held a memory for you all
I'd like to see this poem carved upon a wall
I'd like the new millennium youth that daily passed me by
To understand since time began all men had reasoned why?
If I could choose to live forever and a day
I'd like each child to know I'm glad I passed away
For as I've done before them I'm sure that they will see
That all life is a struggle and death comes easily
And as each candle burns and the new year it does dawn
Take this moment in their lives to ponder and to mourn

If I could choose my last request and every child could see
That following the past is not the way to be
Look towards the future, look towards the sun
For I have had my moment and your time's just begun

Millennium child remember, please don't let us down
For many souls before you lie buried under ground
So keep your candles burning, lighten up the night
Never give up light, never loose the fight
Keep your candles burning, never let them wane
For the next millenniums children will want to do the same.

Joey Joe McGuire 28th December 1999

Refugee Warning

Arise, arise, awaken from your beds
There are bigots all around you, risen from the dead
Don't beg, don’t beg, you'll fuel the blood they crave
For they'll cut you down to size in their charitable way
Awake, awake, tread carefully as you play
For they're waiting for excuses to send you on your way
Compassion, forget it, there is no open door
You're the socially unwanted, the product of the war
They bigoted their own when they hobbled back from strife
And now your backs are bearing targets for the knife
Beware, beware, this warning you must heed
For they grudge the clothes you're wearing
And the food on which you feed
Your heads, your heads, keep them fairly low
For the bigots are awaiting, ready to explode.

Joey Joe McGuire April 11 2000

Nought Point One

Everyone around can see
That you are not the same as me
You are black and I am white
I've been challenged all my life
Ten per cent of one per cent
The difference that we represent
The human eye it tells a lie
You are just the same as I
Nought point one is minuscule
Appearances they had us fooled
A mixture of what you all see
Might make a perfect recipe
You're six-foot and I am five
Tread carefully we will all survive
Please don't move our decimal point
Please don't push us out of joint
For we are happy nought point ones'
Indomitable, creations... ... ...

Joey Joe McGuire 17 May 2000

Freudian Slip

There are those who linger at my garden gate
Hackles all bristling and hearts filled with hate
They watch for a sign to tell them I'm late
Their kangaroo court deciding my fate
The gallows stand awesome, brutal and cold
The lynch mob are gathered, the young and the old
My innocent heart bursting with fright
It seems it's all over, lost is the fight.
A crime so horrific from my very own lips
A statement prolific a Freudian slip
It's hard to be different on a level plain
When all those around you seek profit and gain
My innocent heart misunderstood
By those at my gate baying for blood
I'll swing by my neck on this very day
But I'll stand by my words that gave me away
For I am a man and God made me too
He just made me different, different like you ... ...

Joey Joe McGuire 30 May 2000

(I think this says it all)

<u>My Inspiration</u> (Joey Joe McGuire 13 July 2000)

She was just twelve when I met her
Naïve adolescent of mind
Clutching a book like a letter
That had travelled the distance of time
Unveiled on the pages within
Were the words of a child with no sin
And her presence of mind
As she displayed her rhyme
Left those in her wake with no grin
Her little voice remembered
Embossed on those pages of rhyme
That night when my own days were numbered
She became a new friend of mine
She was the voice of the future
She was the princess of rhyme
Her words would replace mine forever
As an old man gave in to time
She was a great inspiration
A knowledge that when she was done
A little girls new generation
Of poems on that night had begun.

Through Thick And Thin

Poetry is a way of expressing your feelings
Poetry is a way of showing your mind
Not like a story, not like a letter
Poetry is one of its' own kind.
You can write poetry about anything:
Sadness, humour or love,
From a falling leaf to a dying bird
To the air through the wings of a dove
When I was 11 I wrote my first poem
About a headmaster at school
Then dad told me about a man
Who used poetry as his tool
That night I met him at the pub
We talked about poetry for a long time
He wrote poetry as a profession
Mine was in my spare time
He'd written poetry since he was 13
And continued it through his life

He'd never given up hope
In all of his troubles and strife
Through happiness and sadness
Through everything life did bring
Through all his pains and troubles
Everything, thick and thin
He wrote me a poem the next night
About the poetry I would do
Well now, as a gift of thanks
I've written a poem to you.

Rivers Of Red

You certainly exceeded yourselves on that day
Naming forty-nine perverts in your media way
You named them, you shamed them, you left them for dead
And opened the floodgates on rivers of red

Red from the blood of those perverts you named
Relentlessly hunted, hounded and maimed
Why stop just there in naming a few
There are columns of evil joining the queue
Let's pause for a moment consider the fun
The killing, blood spilling
Let's name everyone

Murderers and rapists they all stand in line
Is there anyone living that's not committed a crime
Incest is hiding beside violent abuse
Muggings and torture stand in rebuke
It's easy to see how a tortured mind
Can be a psychological minefield
Ticking with time ...

No one condones anything they have done
But don't make them hide and don't made them run
Try some compassion, understanding instead
Or there'll be more children screaming
And more rivers of red

Hiroshima now long forgotten
And all of the wars from the past
Innocent children down trodden
In Iraq they were all bloody gassed

How many children live on a bowl
Of rice from a cupboard that is empty and cold
None of us innocent, none of us wise
Cowardly hiding behind accusing eyes
Let he without sin cast the first stone
Your media coverage has chewed the wrong bone.

Joey Joe McGuire 25 July 2000
(NOW which newspaper did this go to, three guesses)

<u>With winter gone</u>....

The trees drew breath from the warm fresh breeze
Adorning foliage of fresh, new leaves
Banished was the bitter cold
And life had traded new for old
Forgotten Memories of the Sonne
Omaha, Gold were now long gone
Thoughts of death replaced by life
He'd travelled far, seen awful strife
And in the dewy spring time morn
Memories of his dog were born
That scrawny dog had made him fight
Followed by day, kept him warm at night
He couldn't leave his dog to roam
When it was finally time to travel home
With 'Ninth' Army medal he passed him on
Left his little dog to soldier on
And in the land of dog it ranks
Mightier than one of Rommels tanks
He hopes that dogs have heaven too
As he reminisces in the morning dew.

Joey Joe McGuire August 2000

I'll See You On The Other Side

A Thundering, torrid evening storm
Took your life
And here I mourn
A broken hull, a shattered deck
A loved one lost
Another wreck
The panicking screams were drowned by waves
Giving life an early grave
I still can feel your fingers slip
As you clung for life
But lost your grip
I'll blame myself forever more
Those powerful waves
That tidal roar
Your life, your love, your flesh I'll miss
Your warm and tender loving kiss
None of us from death can hide
I'll see you on the other side
From lonely eyes my tears will drip
When my thoughts are thinking
Of that sunken ship
My love, my love, I'll say goodbye
But I'll see you on the other side.

Joey Joe McGuire
30th September 2000

Advocacy (A Compassionate Plea)

Don't tell me I'm a bird and cut off my wings
Don't say I'm a parrot and tell me not to sing
Don't throw me in a cage and tell me I'm free
Don't stick me in a vacuum and tell me to breathe

Don't say I'm a gladiator and tell me not to fight
Don't tell me it's day when I know it's night
Don't give me a voice that is never heard
Don't cut out my tongue and expect to hear words

Don't give me tears and expect me not to cry
Don't tell me the truth when you know it's a lie
Don't give me a heart that does not beat
Don't ask me to walk and give me no feet

For I am an advocate to those who request
And I'll always deliver my very best
Don't make me a puppet, it's an awful thing
And remember
A bird can't fly without any wings.

Joey Joe McGuire 29 October 2000

Mother Of England

Oh Mother of England so, so sweet
Please grant my wish that we may meet
Oh Mother of England how I laugh
As civilised man weaves his path
Oh Mother of England how I cry
When I see the hatred in his eyes

My Queen, my Queen it hurts so much
For man has lost his tender touch
So many things are now long gone
Those things that made our country strong

The Union now seeks to divide
Lost forever Britains pride
Our coal, our steel have disappeared
Our nation now no longer feared
Our enemies all our allies be
The battles over you must see

My Queen, my Queen I cannot rest
The vultures ripping at my chest
I do not know what I've become
I only know I'm Britains son

Oh Mother of England so, so sweet
Listen how my poor heart weeps
I do not joke, behind the oaks
Lies great unrest from common folk
So note my words my dear, sweet Queen
For visions in the night I've seen

Oh Mother of England so, so sweet
Listen how my poor heart weeps.

Joey Joe McGuire 14 November 2000

A Bitter Pill

It was a bitter pill to swallow alone
Saying goodbye when you'd never been home
Not seventy two years, nor seventy two weeks
Just seventy two hours for your heart to beat

I'd fed you the drops of your mother's milk
And hoped upon hope that your heart would not wilt
Ebony black from toes to your chin
Jaundiced and frail and lifeless within
God had seen fit to take you away
It was a bitter pill that I swallowed that day

Your dust has been spread by the winds of time
But I treasure your memory little daughter of mine
I hope that you're nestled in safety above
And sense my heart aching with fatherly love
I'll never forget your passing away
It was a bitter pill daddy swallowed that day.

Joey Joe McGuire November 2000